W9-BWI-291

Full Summer

The Wesleyan Poetry Program : Volume 95

Frederick Buell

Full Summer

Wesleyan University Press, Middletown, Connecticut

Grateful acknowledgment is made to the following publications, in which some of these poems have appeared: Cornell Review, The Minnesota Review, and A Shout in the Street.

I am grateful to the National Endowment for the Arts for a grant for work upon the poems in this book.

Library of Congress Cataloging in Publication Data

Buell, Frederick, 1942–
    Full Summer.

    (Wesleyan poetry program ; v. 95)
    I. Title.
PS3552.U37F8   811'.5'4   78-25914
ISBN 0-8195-2095-0
ISBN 0-8195-1095-5 pbk.

Manufactured in the United States of America
First edition

For A. M.

Contents

March Sunlight and Cool Air

March Sunlight and Cool Air

Walking one with his arm around the other
       down where I got
              my boat
     I don't take no money with me
             you're crazy!
Hell.
     I don't want someone
               to come along and give me a head job.
Man, if you don't have no money
     they'll kill you.
             With that bald head of yours
anyway, you got no protection.
     Ahhh, look: so they kill me.
At least I got money for the funeral, right?
            Right Eddie?
     — spring blazing up
over middle age.
            Sun drench,
wheat light, rippling, invisible light.
     No history is in this light, seasonless,
of mere exigency.
            No one
      has ever been taken in history
up to the third floor of the Hotel Marlboro
           the sunned drapes pulled
   on the back alley
     why are these contraptions
always so hard to undo
          thinbacked the light
blue sweater pulled off
         jeesus it's cold in here
   no one! Never
       the plump watery-eyed clothcoated
girl at the standup table in the Kosher Luncheon
     talking to her father with cap pushed back and
       sagging jowls
        I see
not one recorded detail in
     this wind
         current

and crosscurrent running ablaze through the society
these breathing impermanent doublearmed erect creatures
the solid
woman walking by the parkfence, heavysoft
rounded belly through the coatflaps,
fleshed cheeks, a cigarette
dangling sideways
from her lips
thoughtful
in 1932
his father died leaving
the family returned to poverty
he was posted in China at the end of World War II
a self-imposed exile, coming back
not knowing what to do selling typewriters
with a curious horror for women
though he talked with amusement
about several affairs
he found himself revoltingly (he said)
driven into later   died as he lived
surrounded by those he needed at arms length —
if she slept with anyone else I
well,
I haven't cheated on her yet
oh wilder than legends this sun brilliantines
our unexamined patch of earth
our earth, our contact with the earth
the flower patches blazing up on it
translucent fleshtone of the cherry trees
pendant dreamfragrant lilac, grape bunched
this dislocated energy coming
back, mindless
the tight
jeans off she told him   look it's
my worst time, you have to use a contraceptive
I know it's unpleasant but that's the way it is
sun pouring in around
the edges, minds
at best like flowers, opening
up in it so wise as to be without effective memory
or separation
this is the way it wanted them
uttering through

the Jamaican woman on the windbuffeted corner
        reading from a green-lined notebook pad
pages whipping about, written on both sides
                    and that is why
        we need the Messiah
                    unheard in a speaking voice
a small blackboard propped on a storewindow ledge
        behind her for drawing a mystical derivation
of mankind
                    a glossy leatherjacketed
impatient policeman leads
        a blind stiff-legged woman
                    white gloves gripping the leather arm
into the traffic
                    no one
        of these has ever lived before

                    the wind-moil on the sidewalk
springwhite sunshine not
        trying to take the freshcool out of the air,
                    being merely light
naked she stood from the rumpled sheets and
        smoothed her small boyish breasts
                    I don't have much up here
            do I? no you
                    do not
oh the humiliating
        intuition we
                    are
        unworthy
                    the intuition is
the longing
        the leprous as the beautiful
        the sordid where the flame of health burns wondrously
        pressed against the Steak and Brew window
                    pallid-faced, merely curious
overlooked—
    Ernie, would you have anything
against it if I worked only four days a week?
        Four days a week?! I know
what it is, you got that other job
                    and now you want to shove me up the ass
    no, you can't work just four days a week

standing in tuxedoes in the dining area, slow
        at three p.m.
no previous life to remember
      dim lit, with wine-red tablecloths & napkins
          —a stoop-backed beggar, coughing protractedly—
a girl with flat-topped hair, though frizzly curls
      shooting out on the sides of a pale
watery and young face
        thin rib-caged
      ribs apparent from her vulnerable back
I'd like you to kiss me there
         whispered in the darkness of the room
      no shame, no shame
the cool outdoor air blowing in the window on them
                  made
    cleverly from the same blood, bowel coils, thigh
      flesh, so that it
        was good
    underneath the greater light hung upon the heliotropic
the splash of red lipstick
         I wonder if someone
    would be interested in telling it
an immigrant, she labored to learn the language
      raised a family and worked to bring
over two sisters and a brother
         a clerk in an accident insurance company
watched her son marry a tramp
      he would come to her in tears, mother, mother
        I love an evil woman, God has punished me
so I couldn't bear it, I was in my changes you know
      and I'd burst out crying, you know?
          my neighbor met me in the
hall, told me I oughta get psychiatric help,
      care like his sister-in-law,
but the next day at work I met a man and paid $2000
         and a friend of his killed her.
I shoulda went to the doctor
      wet eyes behind her thick glasses, wringing her hands
working four hours a day in the prison chapel, it
        is my only comfort bein
      a servant here in His house
        I don't want to die here.

The 15th such spring back for her though it's the only one
        the only one to fire above this wondrous earth
the scarlet-lit thirsts of tulips
                a sexually inflamed bloodroot
            you think it's an accident up ahead?
naah it ain't no accident it's just they're assholes
        no one! no one
                        has loved her still
the shorthaired salesmantype
                short forehead, who grabbed
the heavy woman's shoulders, patted
                    her quickly on the haunch
        see you tomorrow doll, crossed
the street immediately without looking at her
                while she burst out in a laugh whispering
to her friend some of the dope on the guy
        gone in a flash on his business
no one!
                    men standing
            directly in front of the red-tiled pizza counter
bolting down a slice and talking earnestly
        so what is it you see in me anyway, she said
            lighting a cigarette
leaning back, her nipples reddened and puckered with the chill
        no, don't answer that
it's a lousy question
            smiling half cruelly and leaning over
to kiss him
        so he could riposte nothing
as there never is another world
            as there never is another sun
        than over this our business.

Brief Lives

Spring Night Times

I

Beside the subway mouth
green shack low watt
filaments
man with stiff leg
mop bucket with drenched daffodils.

II

Hot moon simmering above the island
light from late night grocery
gates down on store windows
kid loitering by with transistor music
soft ice cream open
block of pale light on the corner
the counterman illuminated, working.

III

A secret kept
smashed front end hood sprung
'72 Chevy carcass
in a H. Hudson turnout
axle propped milk carton
& streetlights across the river.

IV

Man canted against concrete block
wall corner deli almost
summer night
short pants high cork soled
sandals & halter tied
between warm narrow shoulder blades
thighs arched in, seriously kissing.

V

Dark hair & sharp aggressive eyes
applepink polished fingernails
lipsticked Lark cigarette
on a high stool behind the cash register
sexual implication & cynicism.

VI

Movie marquee ablaze
in the thick spring's
hydrocarbons
a slow drift of people beneath it.

VII

In front of the hotel
scotch plaid jacketed red
convention name tag: LEONARD WOSCZYK
inspects the nightwarm crowds.

VIII

Squatting by the front bumper
arc welding, one
bulb lights the shop
hot night, door open,
no deadline for the job.

IX

Walking alone
along the West End
a black guy with ED
stitched on his khaki overalls
wipes some sweat off his temple
beside the river & stars.

X

Woman snoring in the bank
of seats, one standing
with brief silver pants, eyes
painted with a slash of silver
hips cocked beside the subway tunnel
thumbnail against her lips
thoughtful.

To the Season

In the background a siren & carhorns   a team
of sanitary engineers heaving trash in the back hopper
somebody arguing   it is early winter & in general
the personality behind events will disappear   (thank
god for warm rooms & a catholicity of entertainment)
& we all rely on the same thing (more than on each other)

oh it is getting toward the Christmas season   the lights
on the beautiful Norwegian pine at Rockefeller Center will be lit
the four-story displays of streams of bulbs
will jolly up the mercantile part of the city
that woman with legs as thick as sausages & a shock
of strikingly matted thick white hair will doubtless

be back with her three coats & rag bags beneath 42nd St.
(noddling away the evening)   the winter brings
with it a chilly sense of balance   here comes a crushed hat
(I cannot see the eyes) a thick cloth coat though open
and a Shetland wool sweater hanging loosely and no bra
leading her dog & picking her teeth with two fingers

on the Bank Street pier the wind wiping the view of New Jersey
over the ice-grey whitecapped slapping of the Hudson clear
(I tighten up my scarf on it)   And as the nights now lengthen
and begin to cover more of our brief experience   I find I am letting
my attention become other peoples'   for example
the woman riffling through the bills at the bank & sucking

a deep drag on her filter long as a way of refreshing herself
(she's been there over 20 years)   a middle-aged face in a large
oval with thick lipstick   and I find I am in no way content to subtract
from my attention even the rather pettish and affected man I overheard
in a supermarket tell someone he was wearing a Pierre Cardin outfit
his mother a berouged and imperious looking vain woman standing

restlessly by the shopping cart, impatient at being excluded
from the conversation   nor will I omit
the man who flung open the door to a trucking company office,
threw himself one pace outside, then stood stock still
shifting his cigar to a right side cud   evidently unsatisfied
I don't consider myself any the poorer for needing to treat these people

with concern   gradually we're heading toward the solstice
though you wouldn't know it the way the city comes alive at night
and the corner newsstand casts a block of cheer upon the sidewalk
throwing only the most superficial judgment on those who
appear within it walking   turn completely visible   and pass
I think of that in more than naturalistic terms

and it takes some of the spiritual terror away from me
which is a good thing as these nights would like to overwhelm
(with their stars! their stars! spread out billions of miles above
the incidental Hudson) whoever looks at them with the chill
yet radiant, exultant thought of winter, which, minus fear,
is half-bright with the acceptance of existing.

Two Women

Woman thrown out of a bar screaming
hat awry, fierce slash of lipstick
sitting down in a lump
whore ? ya mother was a whore
picking herself up with abrupt
dignity & teetering off among
the blazing lights

thick brown coat, black fur trim her
stocky back dark curled hair
compact in it, swinging a purse
walks, touching the side of her boyfriend,
curiously alert under his shadow.

Poem for a Winter Night

The winter night settled in   snowflakes (no wind) fluttering
down from all corners of the darkness   like the black & white
of a Japanese film in which cherry blossoms are falling
in a courtyard in the past   well, there's much to be had
in the paper tonight   a 71-year-old amputee in London who in fury
at her lodger chased her through a park   in her invalid's car

vengeance, what rage in the old hag's heart   she
smashed & rode over her lodger, then   alas
her car went out of control & spun in narrowing circles, flipped
& burst into flames   Medea could not have had such
bitterness flaring around her victim.   Oh the night!
the snow pitters down inanely in the frozen pause

& maybe in a store open late   a woman stretches a bolt of flare
yellow out across her arm, inspecting it with cocked head standing
there through the display window in the light   I like
at least to think she's doing that   but then I think
the past! The past: before the advent of
the internal combustion engine on the face of the earth

the stardrift closer to the planetary crust   and the Crab
Nebula flaring up in the European & Chinese darkness (reported
both) in 1054   visible above the hard reflecting snowcrust
& windy hovels clustered round the cathedral
the burst of God's fire   signs & wonders
as if above the peasantlike woman who asked me today   you vant

that vash & dri or you vant that folded too   too heavy to be able
to get up easily in the back of her store   who will soon
be vanished herself among them   she is a creature of their range
all those statues on Easter Island erected without eyeballs
or anything below the shoulders thrust in the ground
lines of them staring outwards hieratic at the sun & stars

& waves rolling in softly from 1500 miles away   the nearest land
I admire the civilization that erected them because it did
not ever plan on leaving its little island   it posted itself
as a waiter before the gods of unchanging splendor
that was a sign of fidelity we would   maybe even begin to understand
if we realized that the earth is what it is (an island)

& that the people we love are simply on it looking
well the secret of success he said   is making out a list he
told me of your top priorities and then arranging
your life so that you do not deviate   one jot nor tittle from it
well I did try   I lied about the Crab it occurred in the summer
over the dry sweetness of haytime   amazing those who saw.

Times

Up into Times Square
seasonably cold,
a big winter night
(starry if you could
see it for all
the wattage).

Filtering through
the crowd, one
doddering furwrapped
(white fox) woman
red slash of pomegranate
surreal mouth

pursues her determined
course past me
dead set on the theater
mottled throatskin
jewels   Times
are burning with the
grotesquely vulgar

labia-red COCA COLA
sizzling overhead
one dumpy man
praising the Godfather
II as ''the best Hollywood
movie in the last
15 years'' what

a starved brain
sign of the times
sick that's really sick
some lady is telling
heatedly her man
one of those slick
gritty enduring ones

stirring something in
me to look
at that fierce
mortality that burns here
splendid & unabated
even the broadassed
young cop under his visor

bored, with the reality
touched burning inside
him what stories
of sacrifice & fraternal
sensuality this hierophantic
pomp of human longing.
Oh I feel it

kindling up again in
the counterwoman at Nathan's
her smeared white smock
unbuttoned about the pale
deathwhite throatflesh
the fine backthrust of her
shoulders & the filter cigarette

she sucks for a moment
of observant relaxation
one fingernail tapping
on the counter: the row
of plastic lights around
the glittering box she's in.
What it is

this blazing from
behind the particulars
heavy on their feet
looking up at the bright
white lights I
do not say but enter
into readily

I do not desire it
I do not think it a
property of darkness or
these hieratic lights we've set
up to dim it from view
on the weekend nights
when people are most visible.

Lesser Lights

The dirty interior of the E train rocks   & hurtles us
through the antique tubes   the tunnels under Flushing
I — I cast my eyes around me, curious   just simply
curious for the moment about what time will

in God's name do to these diverse faces   well, age
isn't all that bad, I think, looking at the upturned
kewpie smoothskinned face that expresses someone else's perfection
(I'm glad that I'm not her   what alien internal law

she carries in that blank-appearing look)   & then
staring across the cigarette butts   the lights sliding
by like time within this fading silence of matter   at
a rather dumpy relaxed woman in a pants suit, made

of a silverish thread woven into black   hunkered uncaring
down with tight spit curls and eyes that have
oh what I would call a little glint of uncertainty
shyness even   curious in the center of her self-possession

old enough to have finally won herself an identity
such faces are ones that can pass a judgment on things
now there, there's a person, I think, without nonsense —
& what a sadness it is that the entire

contents of this car   the fertile anxious millions
strap-hanging everywhere beneath this city   the thin
black suited cosmos-black African, twiddling
his fingers with a lovely orange-gold band ring,

the snowhaired woman reading Airport just adjacent to me,
the hawklooked man with the ripe veins on his raised cheekbones,
that in fifty years all these will be forgotten, gone,
swept through the diminishing tunnel of their dying

that is an objective mystery   and with that I think
I personally do not want to be dragged by the hair screaming
in that darkness   (how much do I know that time will really come)
I think that with enough time it will be like traveling

perhaps if there is a God through something that dim ages
have populated amply well before me   not a loss, a loneliness
from people I have not claimed while here   no, but
it will be like a debouching on the Lexington Avenue of another shore

the anxious gathering up of the striped stuffed bags
from Bloomingdale's   the shoulder on shoulder waiting while
the doors release with their regular hiss   the souls
exiting press their way into the crowd of souls

that have been almost impatiently waiting for their return
a shuttle back and forth through matter   perhaps
I am being carried away with the image but
I never could imagine the energy of the dead was gone

without repercussion throughout time   I cannot imagine there could be
no admittance back into the upper world   I cannot imagine the lesser
light of heaven not surprisingly visible above the stairway
nor the opening vista of billions of light years not there without asking.

Celebration

Gusty winter night   streets bare, puddles rippled
Spanish delicatessan open with bleak white light & bare shelves
outside shut off three balls pawn shop sign
man with a green bottle & pulled up overcoat stupid drunk
in front of it   bare red gums, no women & kids anchoring him
the wind blowing shining black hair up off his weatherbeaten cheek
whoaa I walk by him as he almost falls on his hands
splat in a puddle   I turn the corner & lo
Sunday night lonely partiers   there's another
wrestling earnestly on the corner with a metal trash basket
gitoutamywayyousonofawhore   oh the singular celebrations here
among the ice and dimish lights and clear silence
the clean wind that touches me with a chill of a certain sufficiency.

Interior

On this December frozen night my heart is silenced
by the light streaming through the window
of the Orange Julius, the two people
in the broad light sitting at the counter
the woman in imitation leopard coat half
on and off her stool, talking to the somber
counterman, and I outside, frozen in the snow,
beside this matter, this portion shining alienated in the dark.

Snowgathering

Snowgathering in cornicegaps
    orangeglow from Harlem and the Bronx mirrored down from soft cloudbase
privacies and stories told silently
        grew up four blocks from here
brother and father killed in a fire when I was four
    don't remember them
I turned into a real hell raiser.
    The darkness admitting story after story when I was ten I borrowed
        45¢ from my old man went up to the concourse
and sold chewing gum. I bought it in boxes, you know? Sold
        the packs. That was 35¢ profit in those
days, clear. I was ten
    yeah. Proud of himself, wind whipping snow out
beyond yellowlit windows, up about the hotel corner,
        sheet, the taxis slow with lights on.
Hotel 14th story,
    overwarm, couple going in, boxes under arms, door closed,
lock turned.
        Kid had watched his father beat his old lady
over the head with a table leg until he had finished her off.
    No wonder the kid got so fucked up.
Watched his old man open up his mother's skull.
    Queer how the disorders in the retelling become self-containments,
cleared of themselves as the snowfall
    silent and pure into the Hudson, destinies
vanishing without remorse or outcry as they touch the water
    in the distance the GW Bridge lights orange through the veil

oh silence and more silence
    gather around the memories
stilling them
        figure with cigarette in streetlight
galoshes through the bright circlet,
    trudges off around the corner,
        then only the dimlit locked storefronts for a while.

Trainhiss brightsparked into Times Square underground
    through bluepaint turnstile
past Kodak store golddecked underground showcase,
        up with three others the stairwell,
fresh lights and air and snow.

Many oh many wonders here.
    Beggar besnowed under triangular newsbuilding, lights
circling Washington information rapidly around above,
            dejection underneath critical words.
Furcollared woman redcheeked thickset, cigarette out of the mouth corner
    surrounded by theatergoing group, short
hatted and expensively coated husbands on the fringes,
            vigor and excitement beneath the lights
d'ya have the tickets Irv sure sure
    work hard earn your evenings out
o wonder of movie theaters holding out their prurient marquees
            into this silent eternity of snow
this mystery this secret albino darkness mystery

didya ever hear of Louis Horowitz?
    he liked to take pictures an one day
he took a picture of this man in the crowd, ya know?
            That was the last picture he took
as it was a picture of the wrong man,
    cause they killed him.

                    mystery
black kid performing magic card tricks to a small circle
    of passersby paused in the snow
lemme do that one for you again   laugh
    marketplace, this marketplace in such silence

where do they all come from stories and snowcrystals circling downwards
    individually en masse in the darkness
darkness with such mystery of flurried ineffectual activity
            refreshing the mum and deaf world
woman with childbundle, snowglitter on black brilliant eyelashes
    a mystery of individuation and frozenair'd chill pause

d'ya know?
    when she walked out on me it was a relief?
thirty years blown away, and it was a relief?
            as soon as she was gone what I thought would be unbearable just
                                vanished?
lemme tell you, the people who think they know
    who they are don't.
I really thought I knew who I was. Was I surprised!
            You don't know what ya don't need until ya don't have it.

Where do they all come from, whispered
    falling of no more than how things are
snow falling on the ragged edges of the heart,
    queerly calming . . .
crowdburst at door of closing Macy's
            packages and bustle and bright reflecting umbrellas,
breaking in particled voiced disappearances in disparate directions,
    warmfleshed commerce disappearing . . .

Winter Morning

Motes in light shaft, falling
here through Chock Full O' Nuts window
warm across counter & steaming coffee
I in sundrenched noisy diner,
hatted woman with rich
wheatlit purple on her shining skin
talking to friend Lord
ain't no way they gonna get me
to work one more day in that place
they's a bunch of people mixed up in the head
oh yes
fragrance of coffee on winter morning.

Winter Sun

Winter here   from the gutters, long poinards of runoff
sunny glitter   greengrey ice floes in the gutter,
a man with red hood sweater & high galoshes steps
gingerly over it   & the chilly flat white light
falls on the Doric pillars of the Hanover Trust Company
& on the whitehaired crazy guy waving a fist up

and down in the distant warmth. And behind the light?
Don't think, not to think   I will not think
 for a cloud comes over the sun here   across
the visage of the Puerto Rican cab driver with his foot
in the open car door, his eyes closed   who was steeping
in it until the shadow passes up the avenue   & now

looking up the so quickly altered somber street it seems
that, in the chilly umbra beneath several high apartment buildings,
I am passing across medieval Europe below a church
porch   in the snow, a fire, guttering off to the right
I picture two beggars standing against it, puffing & blowing on their hands
in the inner darkness of an earth to be consigned

in horror and glory to the embers   but I know
none who have any more the longing to imagine it this way
& the sun again and the burnt
out Pepsi sign in the window, the sleepy-eyed cash
register girl pouring over a Swedish textbook   looks
out at me suspiciously as I start walking   & the

melting out this afternoon makes me wonder at the feeling
of the cold spring sun burning the first rivulets
through the pine woods in a lost North somewhere
what do the things feel   the crazy ripplings & runnings
where I might live in isolation like a thing
the sun in my face as pure, chilly light and blinking

that is to me a mountain feeling   in an ice cathedral
chunks & boulders of glacial shuddering crush
all my contrarity with their sheer radiance   against
all better reason I see this as blindness surrounding the janitor resting
in front of the Irish bar with his smoking ammoniac
bucket on wheels & mop, leaning against the wall with several

silent buddies   for it is blindness I am positive
for the winter light in its mode of chill and blank celebration
hones in gradually on my recognition   & reverses it
I feel to an unreflectant mirroring   oh in this light
glimmering off car windows & eave ice on the lines of stores
I disappear   I am not I   that cloud has melted into air.

Night Snowfall

Cold air, face cold, lips cold   cloudcover low, red traffic
lights glowing doubly intensely   set of bars, behind it a park
black silhouette of slender tree branches, beside it a young
woman in a tan coat, teased ringlet hair and brilliant lipstick
soft   dark winter to hit us tonight supposedly snow fall

silent through the black treebranch   flesh rich, down stairs,
row of low watt yellow bulbs, warmth, people lined, digging
in pockets   hotdog stand, three kids leaning against the counter
lowceilinged subway platforms electric lit   then subway car
white shadowless light people sitting, close, staring openly

around each other   you let me look in that the angry
woman across from me, her man with his feet shoved out from
the subway bench looking off to the corner, bored   a ripped
jacket on   comeon you let me look prods him, finally he
lifts one side withdraws a thin fold of patent leather which

she scours, opens, searches intently inside, holds upside down
unbelieving   how close we are across this brilliantly lit aisle
and how close to the middle-aged woman with furcollar coat blue
reading glasses rouged cheeks   seated just beside me, across
from her a white workman with Germanic haircut, deathly

pale skinned with square toed shoes staring nowhere blankly
and the whisper behind us   a whisper a secret, as if a love
love me   the whisper behind this executive who seems
to me a perfection of his type, hornrimmed glasses, striped
suit, neatly tanned face, a sheet of legal paper underneath

his hand, this late, behind the rush hour crush, singled
out for me with the light upon him   how secret this is is
revealed to me now in the interchange walking by the three
self-concerned fixed in the righteousness of what has been
done to them   mean faces with cigarettes   cruel and laughing

with unconcern for what creates them pain   and now this
black man with the knee-length checked overcoat, elbow on
the lunchshop counter, cream brimmed hat tilted askew, gold
rings on three of his fingers   he laughs, and claps a friend
between the shoulderblades between   I see the stringy

reddish haired waitress with matter of fact unmoving mascaraed look
has just finished serving them   how secret this whisper I
think   none of us hears it and yet all of us
are insistently and quietly surrounded by it   now in the turnstile
snow doubtless beginning upstairs   closepacked with others I hear
I think I hear it   pressed by the frail shoulder of a bundled woman.

Morning Thoughts

The sun is mantled by pewter clouds—
it blazes from behind them with silvered light into
the canyons between buildings
I notice it over my shoulder as a monitory

energy as I walk
minute after minute into my coming future—
into the underground,
head bowed, reading among newspapers—

stirred, looking up, catching sight
of the station sign,
climbing out, up the stairs, into
the sunlight again thirty miles away—

into the bus and to my job—
oh in my mind clouds similarly of dreams
I wish I could divest myself of,
become unconscious as the light shimmer

on the stubbled pale cheek of the bus driver
touched by the silvery radiance—
on the elderly woman with beehived hair
her lined mouth set about its lipstick

motionless now, unvoluble—
on my cheek as well pressed against the cold window—
oh god! what unreal hopes burn inside me
blazoned on the furrowed brows of my hollowed face,

clouds to the pressing fire of my heart,
ablaze with its conflicting desire and feelings—
rooted in this uncertain weather,
I am on fire with premises I cannot discern—

Ancient World

Oh give me the sun! the epic sun of actions
    daylight flooding the city and globeface,
actions individuated and veiled in the megolopoli of survivals,
        as a dayrise behind an upland secondgrowth woodland,
a marl of convoluted trunks and branches, luminous with hopes—

warm morning down populous Broadway,
    glint of broken green bottles flashing on gutter and sidewalk,
facement of the trashy Carlton Arms hotel,
        walking past a man steering his steel wheelchair,
battery propelled (Diehard Powercell)
    a brilliant redlipped smile on his rounded and loosejowled face,
down to the theater advertising CRY RAPE vacant and unvisited
        (how much the dawn is more wonderful)

what I passed were four policemen subduing a thinarmed man
    yelling incoherently,
one with his knee in the small of the back, fighting to get the handcuffs on
        what power in that wiry craziness—
turned over I saw he was half sodden, in his fifties
    an old man, violent and uncaring of consequence—

what happened was clear a block later:
    a squarejawed woman with tropical features had beaten
        him off an elderly German he had lunged, reasonless, onto,
extracted from him a 6-inch clasp knife, unopened though—
    in the ancient world people moved through their lives bearing weapons
so too him, with the daybreak of the earth in his mind,
    yelling and vaunting doubtless all the way to the precinct and cell
not to be submerged in this massive world,
    not him.

A Single Night

Summer darkness
crowd sprawled around
    the parkfountain's edge,
the lit glow of cigarettes,

dog splatting through
the water
    tensely to retrieve
a chucked can

hey man, come on, leggo,
short guy with battered hat
    his arm twisted
cruelly behind his back

get the fuck out of here
before I break it
    girl talking
to two friends

yeah, well you know why?
He said just as he was leaving
    he got a call, this kid
had threatened to kill his parents.

He said he had to get
written permission to enter
    the building, you know?
The owner or someone,

then he and his partner went
over there, and the parents
    they told him the kid
was locked in this apartment.

He said when they got in
they saw this kid:
    this huge, monstuh kid
bigger'n they were,

they tried to get him
in the handcuffs, you know?
    Both of them,
like they could only

get one of the kid's arms in the cuffs,
he was stronger than both of them.
    While they were fighting the kid,
his parents must've

reconsidered or something,
you know, they saw their kid
    being beaten up on
and got second thoughts,

I can understand that.
What happened was that the parents
    got in on it—
he said the man went

for his partnuh, and the woman
went for him, ripping
    their clothes and everything.
You know, I was really

surprised when I saw him.
He was really young
    good looking and sincere,
not what you'd expect.

He said he'd answer any
questions about the law,
    somebody asked him
about corruption.

He said you take an oath
when you become a detective
    he said he'd arrest anyone
even if it was a cop who did anything wrong.

In other words
the impression I got from him
        was that he was
a frank, honest cop

who would arrest anyone
even if it was his brothuh.
        Sitting around the fountain,
moonslice and planet overhead

her breasts high behind the blouse
throwing her hair back,
        looking around,
see what happens.

In the Midst

Sunburnished roadways
   storefronts with smashed glass
                abandoned barricades
kids leaning on them, drinking
   t-shirted and slouched in the lassitude
of affected ease in ready angers,
   in a world of damaged artifice
      (Ya know what they did to her?
They cut her throat and threw her on the tracks)
           o heat in which
sunparched mouths thirst for rare waters
   refreshment of the flesh

exiting couple with groceries celery
   askew out of the bag oi
                it's a goddamned furnace out here

actually in the midst of this debris of
   spirit and furniture—
cheap hamburger store with window open because of heat
     man inside flipping the unnourishing patties
T-shirted, armpits circled with sweat—
   trash circulating down from the Bronx, blowing
downtown, say along the western avenues, eddying in
     circles near the Battery, then migrating uptown on
the other side—
   actually there is much
for quiet to wonder at—

the fine back muscles, straining, triceps
   sweat glistening in the heat,
ribs of youth tendoned beneath the shoulderblades as one
     climbs up to a building ledge retrieving
something metal glinting lying there
   —that body was handsome

much weightier matter for awe as well
    the man waiting potent and dangerous
against the side of the car in which
        a woman, nicotine stained fingers and upset face,
little boy frozen in the back, sat,
    until a fatting middle-aged man exited;
tumbled through the crowd, he was thrown against the car,
        shot first in the shoulder,
then with the blind cry you raped my wife
    shot pointblank five times in the face—

there was one child whose life would thunder
    with the violence of history

Margin

The brilliant orange arc lights, the blinking red TRUST
   TEXACO PRODUCTS beacon, then a man, one story high
   in a velvet sportcoat, ENGLISH LEATHER MEN'S COLOGNES
   the jammed road slowly rising to an elevated section then
   turning gracefully, and winding down to the mouth
   of the Midtown Tunnel, then Manhattan, aglow.

To the left of me a philosophical cabby, chin propped
   heavily on his hand, his fare in the darkness behind him.
   And the man in the Lincoln Continental, his tie
   open at the throat, gold rim glasses, pressing
   his head back against his headrest, despite
   his affluence, frozen with us in the traffic.
   He is chewing gum, almost thoughtfully, it appears.

To my right, looking neither to his right nor to his left,
   in a little battered rambler, old and out of place,
   an exhausted middle-aging face, eyes very
   heavylidded, one who seems a petty accountant or such, but
   an expression—as if centuries of history have been
   inscribed by patience in his face . . .

All at a crawl down to the tolls, a white clock face
   with thick black hands reading illuminated 6:15
   I glimpse behind it two policemen standing, talking across the cars
   and (the hair raising on the back of my neck) I feel something is
   pondering and dreaming of us, upon this margin.

Thunderstorms along Manhattan

Going through the Holland Tunnel, the smutty roof, green
　　lane guide lights, and the blue wall signals
　　like the runway lights in airports, cobalt blue,
　　solid red band reflected on the walls from taillights

and above on the freeway the one and two story row
　　homes of New Jersey, rusted copper topped churches, spires,
　　to the left the World Trade Center lit up, its top
　　literally in the bottom of a massive cloud,

a heavy thundercloud rolling over. The magnificent
　　cloudscape, over Manhattan as if force collecting about
　　the poles of the Trade Center, over New Jersey lightning,
　　on the right the clouds thinning, cumulus below.

Sunflowers on a bridge, deep black center, golden leaves
　　radiating from the center slightly drooped,
　　bent geometric suns on the concrete siding.

The pearl strings of lights across the flat wetlands,
　　the sky that is striated grey, lower becoming brushstroked,
　　down the absolutely straight turnpike, Newark runways,
　　the planes coming down opposite in a distant line.

The plane landing lights on hanging in descent,
　　oh God off to the right the sunset, a Holiday Inn
　　in the far distance, green neon sign, another motel
　　the top of it silhouetted, behind immensely

empurpled sky, crack at the edge of creation, fire
　　coming through it, energy across the perfectly flat land.
　　Looks through us, profound attention,
　　wan headlight tracks in the sallow twilight.

I glance at the man traveling next to me, 65
　　mph even with my car, inhales his cigarette, cracks
　　the window top to put it out carefully

face tracked over with fatigue at the day's end
   tie pulled open and coat rumpled,
   his lungs expelling the sweet smoke.

His a sensual face although possessed with the caustic
   energy of the New Yorker in business, this
   intensely serious workaday smoking urban
   island outlined in the August thunderstorms,

profound and greengrey variable power overhead.
   He could tell you something about people,
   I can tell you something about the power
   of their history, looked into by the red

slash that cuts level, lengthened shadows, cross the wetlands.
   I can tell you as the gulls settle onto
   the channels by the throughway bedding,
   splashing the darkening salt water about their wings.

I can tell you as I pass a Puerto Rican changing
   tires on a jacked up car, a Continental Trailways
   bus with large red stripe running the flat length
   of the straightaway, and the EXXON sign glowing in the air.

I, in this wave of radiance, this rush of cars
   speeding the same direction athwart the sunset,
   community of orange light, half dissolved in the luminescence,
   the bashed hind end of the car with black

arms cradled on the windows, its taillights hanging
   half askew, an exhilaration in the wave of energy,
   I can tell you of the power here
   cast from humankind in flow.

Questioning

The polished floor of the highceilinged terminal,
the orange illuminated Benrus clock above,
the lines of travelers, the black
man standing with his coat upon his arm, his beaded brow,
in front of the Hoffritz Cutlery window, the light from it
falling to illuminate without details,

the mist removing from sight the buildings far across town,
the vanishing behind the lines of traffic lights,
dropping off the horizon into sleep,
the business, dominion, and rituals that have lost themselves in time.

Passing through the watery fog of the buildings in the seaclouds,
the large aluminum milk tanker with three vents in the polished top,
and the flatbed truck with compacted bodies of different colored steel,
both running superfluously into Manhattan with the others,

and the taxi that careened past me, the front seat with
a Latin woman with brilliant red scarf, the back with three men —
one with hatbrim up all around, one with a comb in his Afro,
and one hidden from me — all with cigarettes out of the front of their mouths
tailgating the cars in front — driving alone I wonder

do we know anything out there desires our fame?
That something shall not forget the taste of how things were?
That it shall not forget the overpass beneath which we are driving,
in the tense New York early morning dawnlight off to work,
crowded with the others, eyes sleepy and radios on the news —

or that it shall not forget the elderly white man, descending the steps
of the loan office, his windnipped pinkish skin
knotted at the brows in an introspective frown, clumsy
hands lighting and placing in his mouth a deepdrawn cigarette
(on the first day of New York winter, in its chill and singularity)?

And shall it forget the gas station in Newark, the Puerto Rican
with a diamond patterned hat, a black shirt with a white
stripe down the arm, short, stocky, large-cheeked,
arguing vehemently with a towering milk-brown-colored black,
in a cutoff blue sweatshirt, a pencil stuck in the back of his hair?

And shall it forget the man, proud as the hierarchs of Babylon,
pushing his trashfilled wheelbarrow steadily down 8th Avenue,
his coarse torn shirt, his stoop, his disappearance among the stars?

Then what is it in the two women talking here in the subway
the one with frenetic hand gestures and chewing gum,
the listener grave, her brown-polka-dot dress
and red formal hat erect beside the black window
the darkness rushing behind their earnest communications,

and what is it in the slightly
corpulent businessman, flying in from L.A., with
black shoes and golden buckles, stitched pockets in his suit,
wraparound dark glasses, exhausted with his elbow propped
and chewing gum, his mind deciding on the world with the speed
of his confident jaws, running a finger around his tight shirt collar?

And in the man glimpsed momentarily,
his chin propped wearily in the lit window of a metropolitan bus,
framed by the greenish light, and gazing out, profoundly serious,
through whose eyes I look back into the millions of dawns upon this world?

And am I not witnessing a secret in the freshened early rainmist
the small, southern, overcoated black man, some 70 years old,
walking with his face contorted in discomfort, querulous,
nearing the men working at the underground garage,
brightening suddenly with eagerness, with the promise of talk?

And is it not from some impelling that I am intent upon
the man hunched over a burger and a coke in the White Tower,
the counterman leaning with his back on the plexiglass cabinet,
holding several pastries, working still at 12 p.m.?

And the derelict with the running eyes and incessantly
soundless moving lips, and the thickfaced aging woman, her hands
thrust beneath the flaps of a green quilted overcoat,
talking in the pallid dusk to a gas station attendant
(I see he is excited by something, he touches her on the arm)

and the workman, sleeping, head thrown back against the colored wall,
his mouth open, subway rocked with hair tousled behind him,
jolted in weariness, is there not something to be revealed behind?

And behind you, butting your cigarette
out with a nervous gesture, turning around in your chair,
looking about in the barlight, shouldering your purse suddenly,
and lurching toward the double door?

And you, restrained by the patrolman,
your shirt torn open, your chest beaded with sweat and your eyes
rolling with terror and anger, the blood from the side
of your face streaming, as you stand shaking and gawked at
in the crowded 24-hour emergency room of the hospital?

And you, standing with foot pushed forward on its heel,
looking at your red polished nails and glancing up
at your friend, a darkfaced woman with an orange scarf on her hair?

Pale, balding, folds of skin upon the back of your neck,
a brown and white checked jacket from which your belly protrudes,
you pass me suddenly in the crowd at the theaters in Times Square;
profoundly mysterious, you hold a paper bag
with thumb and forefinger at one end, stand secret and wide-eyed.

And in a restaurant I overhear your friend remark to you
that her sister was blind in one eye and goin blind in the othur
oh god, you said with disgust, sitting in your brief fur coat,
darkly mascaraed eyes, chewing gum with your alert realism.

And though you are alone in the dim light of the bus waiting room,
folded up, diminutive in your chair, a small
ragged flight bag carefully positioned between your feet,
though on your face is written exhaustion,
I gaze at you closely, and hope though helpless that you not disappear.

Full Summer

Full Summer

Out of the heat haze steaming off the lines
    of passing vehicles,
out of the parkbench sunstruck woman
        with a face from El Greco, lined with dark
                slashes of shadow about ascetic thin cheeks,
whispering with flat declarative earnest sibilant whispers
    into the ear of an attentive companion, her eyebrows
        plucked and her face pointed in a frown,
out of the traffic where the girders of a bridge arise
    on broad asphaltic stanchions, where two boys in fatigue jackets
and shining dusky faces disappear in collusion underneath one
    out of its own abundance it comes.

For the life cried to its foundation, cried without knowing it
    cried from the streets of the gaudy Puerto Rican stores,
the pride of the mother leading her three children, the eldest
        daughter with her soft hand on her shoulder,
tiptoe, looking down with her at the merchandise, cried
    from the line of moviegoers, waiting, the one
man punching in camaraderie the arm of his friend,
    their two wives talking intensely just behind,
and cried of coming to this country and marrying a West Indian
    who has his son now, they all lied to the judge,
        her and her mother, and I am alone here without friends
what could I do? I only want to take my son away from her
    and go back to Teheran, but the judge doesn't listen
to me only to a woman, women! They have no sense
    of right and wrong, only what they can lie to get
cried in the multiloquent darkness, the summer
    night with the late gaud of the open liquor store:

the tiniest spot on your forefinger is the woman
    thrown from the window and bursting in her blood below,
the cartilage and naked bone,
    one sinew of your arm the one-legged girl who humps
in an eternal persistent rhythm canewise across the corner
    a bright yellow kerchief on her head,
your neck shaft is like the righteous black
    woman who guarded her twelve year old son in the cut-rate clothing store,

your teeth are like the bedroom windows beneath which
        the silence is punctuated by scarcely audible whispers and laughter,
            in the shade of your arms the Puerto Rican
bars light up with the roses and greens of the Latin jukebox,
        the couples moving among each other with tender dangerousness.

The shaft of your leg is the silent
        endurance of the abandoned,
in the lashes of your eyes
            the man that the cops asked to open the door
                Juan so I can come in for a glass of water
if you come in for water I must die
        well then, I won't, because that is an awfully high price to pay
but five seconds later they heard the shot of the gun in the mouth,
        and the breath that moves across your lips the composed whispers
of the two wrinkled women on the bench in the park.

Your loins are the brilliant sunrays glittering
        almost tangibly in the faces of the four
determinedly aggressive youths prowling the sidewalk with their warclubs,
            mixing anarchic tenderness and violence in their lives,
        the sternness of your brow is the six year old child
tortured and thrown off the roof of a tenement by her peers,
            the composed intelligence of your eyes
is the delicate manliness of the Puerto Rican boy I saw walking
        by himself along the bars of the filthy park
in the pale vacant sadness of the Easter morning.

        Oh body of this world
of the old negro woman laboring querulous-faced up
        the gritty electric-smelling maw of the noon subway, breathing heavily,
a parcel of lambent orange flowers in her hands,
        of the emotions
that play across the figure of the man, seated
                over the greenhued counter in an open-doored
hamburger joint, the colored advertisements flashing
        above his volatile face, change, change.

For the heart's blood pumping in your superhuman frame
        is traffic clattering down the distant avenue,
the strength and proportion of your torso is the orange
            afternoon light hued forever

on the doorway in which a redcracked squalid stunted
         man with ripped trousers and wind-hardened skin is hunched,
                  a bottle of Miller's ripe gold by his battered hand,
         and the brawn of your lower back is the Latin in black
slapping a long flashlight in his hand as he sits
                  beneath the tawdry shadow of a $1.00 movie marquee upon
the rebuilt front hood of an old Chevrolet, yelling
         banter to three friends against the wall.

The discharges of your neurons are the nervous racing subways,
                  freighted with the information of their transitory lives
vanishing into darkened tunnels to which the end is forgetfulness,
         the aura about you is the mysterious
and dangerous love that cradles the proximate millions
                  climbing the stairwells breathing with music and words
yelling down the bannisters the extremes of their world,
         and in the hair of your secret places the fierce
                  hands clutch a masculine back
the face from below transfigured in its concentration.

         And I say this of you
nor I but the stocky bald crude vital clerk who looks
                  at me incredulous when I argue with his price,
the whore on 8th and 32nd, the black from Alabama with a soft
         look on his face as he converses on a park bench with his friend
and the waiter with sweated
         lucent brow, with thick chopped and
quizzically irritated staring, who repeated incredulously whas that? at
                  I isk you three time eef you have zaccherin, coming
from a flourwhite cane-clutching woman whose bloodshot
         creased eyes were on the counter level, who refused the milky coffee,
and hobbled out bitterly complaining to the sundrenched streets.

All voices coming out of the thousand-creviced city,
         the crash of voices the startled outcries in a crowd,
         the voices of the pleading whisper, the woman
with a drinking problem in the family court, the judge
         threatening to legally orphan her damaged children,
         and the voice of the stocky booted workman
roaring OK NOW GET THAT TRUCK THE FUCK OUT OF HERE
above the ratchety idling motor, the double doors just bolted tight behind.
         The voice of the technicians

in shirt sleeves holding official clipboards,
    the small voice of the child asking where mommy went to,
the voice of the overburdened bureaucrat explaining
        why this is not the required form
for certifying tax payment on a second hand vehicle,
    for the third and not the final time.

And out of the locked apartment in which a septuagenerian
    who has outlived his wife and his children and friends
feels himself moving at last toward the darkness that claimed them,
        a speaking darkness, luminous with Ida's runny eyes
and tender mouth, perhaps in the end void of terror,
    out of this arbitrarily calculated twentieth century
out of this time too, these voices come.

They come to build a world, a place for the street hung
   in haze, shouts from the corner, the dim subsistence
of the Chin Doon Chinese Hand Laundry, the flat white sanitation
     truck working the length in the warm green light,
the corner deli, staffed by the man who remembers
   the World War II freighters, the slow immigrations,
the telltale tattoo on the wrist. To build a world in which
   mockery toward the meanest of creatures, the Pole
whose attic loft was filled from floor to ceiling with
   packratted rags, the fire officials ordering
the life anxiety of the man, bleary-eyed, un-
   communicative, to be cleaned out and burned
(we couldn't get the guy to go on welfare) while he wept
   in the first floor entryway at the workmen hauling
the bales down into the metropolitan truck—to build
   so mockery and patronizing alike are affronts
to the solid, breathing certainty of what exists—
   this is a distributive world of love

   for what lives and is more than righteous, what lives
ablaze both within and with the whole. The young
   Jewish girl from the Bronx, confused,
her tentative face lined with fear,
   incapable of finding many words, trying
in the park sunlight though haltingly to convince
   a hostile man of the Word of the New Universalists,
three men in conversation, a woman nodding by them
   her child asleep on newspapers spread out on the bench
the three leaning together, yeah, that brother sure needs help,
   cause he's got trouble on his mind,
and the girl in the bar who went on about that mother
   who had the villa in Northern Italy, the butler
the servants and all that shit. I told him, now look, baby,
   don't lay that genteel crap on me, I don't need it,
     I am not impressed.

The pair of hands and the helpless ingratiating mouth
   can you spare a dime from a doorway, the
broadbeamed closecropped darkhaired old woman,
   catching sight of him and passing, asking
of the other—him, what'd he ask you for? A dime?
   These days they ask me for quarters. Inflation, y'know, and laughs.

Well, there's one in the subway station on Broadway,
        they call her Bloody Mary, she was written up
in the Times. Me, I'm from the neighborhood,
    I see her every day: she's got ulcers on both legs
they're swollen up this big, you know?
        well, she's a real shock if you don't know her,
but I see her every day, sometimes she shares
    her money with the others, that's Bloody Mary.
Every so often the cops come and take her off to a hospital.
    To build a place for all things, all possibilities in the sun.

But why should we address you —
    why should we push our hats back and look up
at the dense cloud cover, the summer rains blowing
        slowly in over the crowds in brightly colored clothes?
    Here is the legless man, asleep in his steel
wheelchair, a beer can caught between his remaining thighs,
        dozing on the busy streetcorner, his
reddened stubble face canted over like a ragdoll's
    a police whistle hanging about his vulnerable neck
(in case someone tries to rob him of the chair)
        here is the T-shirted black man,
with a blue Con Ed hard hat, washing his hands
    at a fire hydrant at 5:30 by the street dig,
several teeth missing from his smile at a woman,
        here is the hotweather garb, the Indian blouse
caught underneath her breasts and billowing over her hips,
    pointedly not looking at anyone as she walks,
this flesh as rich and supple as a poppy bank in the wind.

    The Jewish woman, deep circlets under her
    ironic-all-the-days-of-her-life exiled pragmatic face,
thinwaisted, brittle, though a large
        patch of glaring red lipstick as if
to say mere prettiness is a vanity and chasing the wind,
    grudgingly waiting on the corner beneath an opposing light,
        the loud breath of conga music from
the empty bar, with the alert and made-up
    Puerto Rican woman bartender, ready
        with folded arms for a night of business and conversation,
the man in the truck back beneath the wrecked building,
    methodically crashing window frames and glass
into the loud debris he is compacting,
        and the thin-jawed elderly sunless
white with flushes of arterial rose Scotch gentleman,
    standing with tightlipped highland burliness by the curb.

In the green-grey haze, hanging over the view up north,
        the working millions, the queues of automobiles,
the dim interior of the bar, empty, at noon, save
    two people discussing a suicide from Brooklyn Bridge
(two weeks ago one tried it and he didn't die,
        they hauled him out — the bartender on his elbows,

65

a cigarette and drink between his hands—well,
    you know I guess it all depends on how you enter the water)
with the men out of work on the muggy afternoon, stooped
        over the sidewalk in their undershirts
holding a fist with folded dollar bills bristling from it
    tanned backskin and a yell as the dice fall,
one walking away shortly in obvious regret and increased tedium
    a bitter scene brooding somewhere later around him,
and with the teenage Puerto Rican mother, hipshot, holding
        her blue-blanket wrapped child guardedly in her wiry arms,
the millions of people across whom in marriage
    divorces and affairs, doorwells, rooms with hot open windows,
small booths in a cellar Alhambra, the wave
        of love rises, commingles, stirs, and becomes.

But what lies behind this world, as if
    the colors of streetlamps at night, the luminescent
coils hanging in front of restaurant and bar, or those
      of the faces lined with the shades of tanned
orange, rich empurpled black, were living harbingers,
    dropping a pile of pine boards on the sidewalk in the sun?
What 'awake and shout, ye that dwell in the dust' is heard
    in the bloated red face of the woman derelict
seated in her squalor and talking
      to her friend, an orange cat, lying in the shopping cart of rags?
What moves behind the deckhand on the tugboat,
    waiting in the bows to loop a heavy yellow hawser
over the water and around the stump of the floating barge,
    and what realizes itself in the throw, as the
vessels grind together with a heavy jolt?

In the face of the black subway trainman, guiding
    the cars through the labyrinthine underground, blossomed
with flashing white lights and red and green signals,
      coming on the loudspeaker at the station, laconic and nasal,
all right, who's the wise dude that's got his arm in the doors,
    working the night shift from 12 on to 8
the luminous darkness and soft metamorphosis of the species,
    the vegetative humor of their transformations,
in the heart of the Russian Jew, seated in his doorway
    watching the avenue filled with its traffic,
watching with the pained love of its inadequacy, the yearning
    flares around him of the bowels of the Shekhinah,
for all those transactions and transpositions going on under the sun,
    in the young Spanish featured man with his dangerous chic
of bright hand-decorated shirt and his proud frown,
    the infinite tenderness of the lily, and the rich savage feminine,
and the moral dilemma of the aquiline white pedestrian,
    walking slowly with his head down, brooding,
trying to work clear the pattern in his life,
    certain of order, unsure as to his place in it,
the pressure of his taking stock is an echo
    of an unsettled dim roaring in his private mind.

The world of history, history: the gridwork of streets
    by the oceans, mercantile streets, ringing with pasts,
strange computer, sorting beneath the heavens
        people and their lives, where what does not circulate
is not remembered, this one brief time on earth.
    On the sidewalk, in front of the packers' overhang,
people skirt the scarlet pool of the butcher's delivery,
        the whitejacketed carrying the carcass on his bent
back, held with tongs, into the airy building.
    Or in front of the funeral home, two slickly
dressed employees, carefully groomed, come out in the sun
        one lights a cigarette and puts his foot up on a hydrant,
talk about the semifinals, snap the smoke away and go inside.

    The woman with a knotted frown yet wineblue
neck choker, almost luminous in the dim sunlight,
        the tall stifflegged squareshouldered black,
her jaw square, half pentecostal righteousness and
        half deeplined agony, walks, soldier erect,
past the battered trash cans, or the tall cop who leans against
        a wall with his buddy—when my wife and I were out
in the badlands last summer, you know? I saw this
    little whitetailed ringhorn goat and parked the car
right under the cliff. That little bugger sat up there
        and went like this with his hoof, pushing
pebbles down on the windshield! My wife said come on
        let's get out of here, but—Hey Joey! long time no see
and the cop drew himself up guardedly: Well. What are
        you doing back here, glaring down at the man.

History: the sun burns its way clear of the haze,
    the pavement seems to lighten up from within,
here and always, the man with bare back and luminous skin
        lying with his shirt off on a bench, a paper
over his head and upper shoulders—the sunlight!
    on the throat and collarbones of the girl in the diaphanous
Moroccan blouse, her eyes half closed and content walking,
        allowing the pockets of shadow, the second
floor walkup where a man kisses the wrinkled
    stomachflesh of his girlfriend, her hands gripping
his shoulders, holding him there
        their clothes scattered over the dressertop and chair

the sunlight burning over the thousand gas stations
  battered cars with hoods up and men lounging in grease
stained uniforms dreaming across the streets for an hour,
    the sun upon them standing, like a wheatfield
ripe and never to be harvested by man.

No violence, no love that has not been enacted,
  and is not equally as new, the light on the face
of the leathery-skinned woman with ash hair who can remember Sicily,
    the dry fragrant grass and the rock strewn hills,
the man just released from Riker's Island with his cardboard
  soled shoes, the paralysis patient, in his glistening
steel wheelchair on the hospital sunroof, the roar
    of the air-conditioning unit behind his claywhite face,
the kid in the torn denim jacket, riding the steel between
  two subway cars, the hot dirty rush of the tunnel
with its flickering colored lights sweeping by on either side,
    twenty miles of haunting and abrupt clatter,
and the man taking an elbow smack in the face at the playground basket
  dropping down and yelling shit man, you do that again
an' you're a dead motherfucker, wiping the sweat and blood away.

Into history—the sun sinks, pewter colored, above
  the river, slightly reddened, the salt rank
seawrack smell blowing in over the end of the level pier,
    three couples on the end in the late afternoon.
One girl stands up, her black hair blowing, hipshot
  her arm on the shoulder of her crosslegged friend, who
remains looking inward. She leans down to him, says
    something that is lost in the wind,
then straightens, rather thickset and flabby at the waist,
  and raises her arm to her bare neck to flick
her head back, so that the hair blows away from a smooth
    cheek and shoulder—while the sun, eloquent luminary,
visible to us as to the ancient Judean deserts,
  as to the rich silence of the pre-Columbian Great Plains,
    settles in front of her, going to prepare a novel world.